AIR MINISTRY.

Directorate of Research.

I.C. 676

REPORT

ON THE

JUNKER ALL-METAL SINGLE-SEATER MONOPLANE, TYPE D.1.

JULY, 1919.

H. R. BROOKE-POPHAM,
Brigadier-General,

Director of Research.

The Naval & Military Press Ltd

JUNKER MONOPLANE.

Published by
The Naval & Military Press Ltd
5 Riverside, Brambleside, Bellbrook
Industrial Estate, Uckfield, East Sussex,
TN22 1QQ England

Tel: +44 (0) 1825 749494
Fax: +44 (0) 1825 765701

www.naval–military-press.com
www.military-genealogy.com

AIR MINISTRY.

Directorate of Research.

I.C. 676

REPORT

ON THE

JUNKER ALL-METAL SINGLE-SEATER MONOPLANE, TYPE D.1.

JULY, 1919.

H. R. BROOKE-POPHAM,
Brigadier-General,

Director of Research.

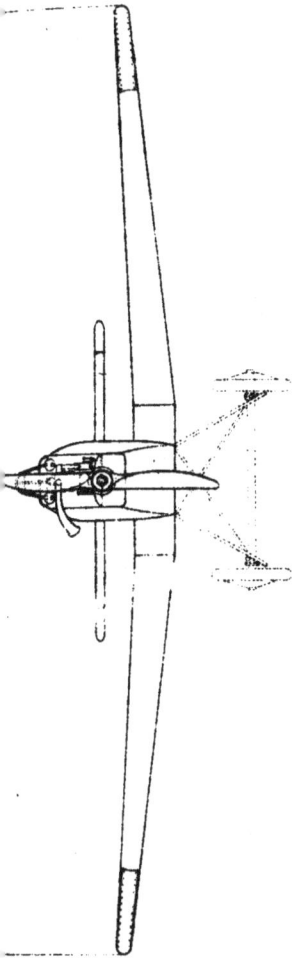

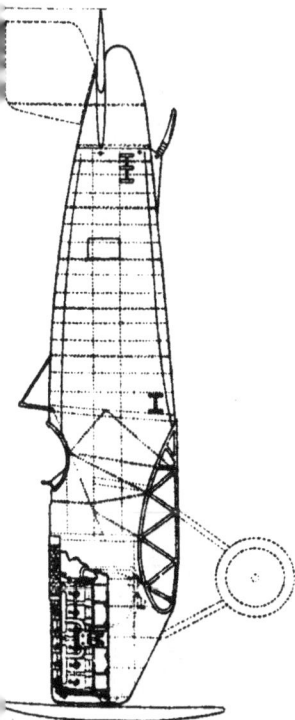

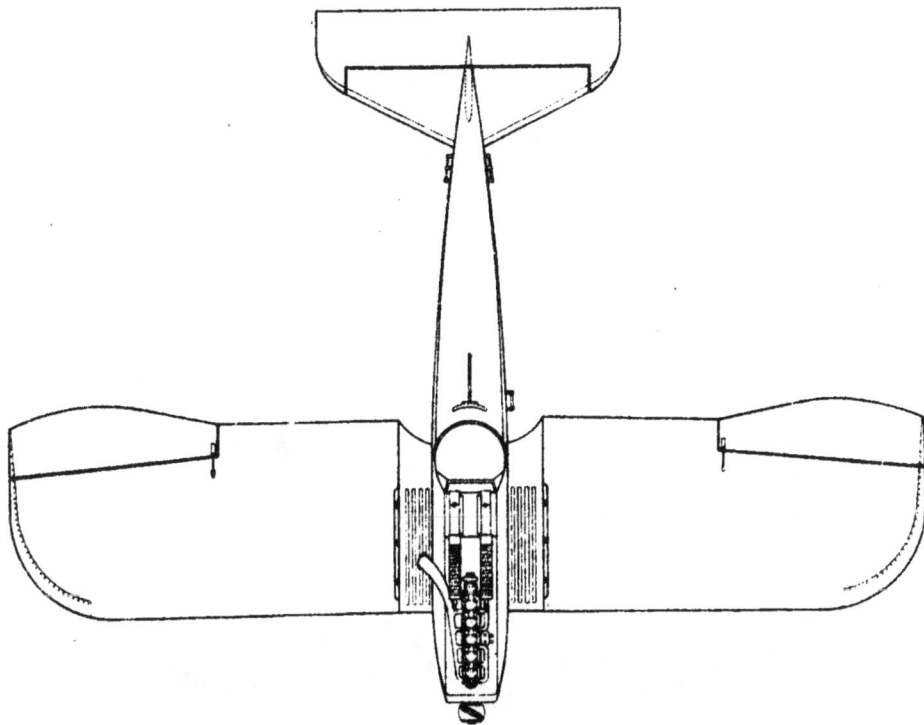

JUNKER - ALL - METAL - MONOPLANE.

TYPE D.I.   180 H.P. MERCEDES.

Scale of Feet

	F.	I.
LENGTH OF PLANE	12	3½
CHORD AT ROOT	5	11½
LENGTH OF AILERON	6	6¾
MAXIMUM CHORD OF AILERON	1	11½
SPAN OF CENTRE SECTION	4	7
MAXIMUM HEIGHT OF BODY	4	1½
MAXIMUM WIDTH OF BODY	2	5
DIAMETER OF PROPELLER	7	2½
DIHEDRAL OF UPPER SURFACE OF WINGS (ESTIMATED)	3°	
ANGLE OF INCIDENCE (ESTIMATED)	1°	
SPAN OF ELEVATOR	9	10
CHORD OF ELEVATOR	1	9½

THE MIDDLE ILLUSTRATION IS FROM A GERMAN PHOTOGRAPH. THE UPPER AND LOWER ONES ARE FROM PHOTOGRAPHS TAKEN IN BELGIUM OF THE ABANDONED MACHINE.

REPORT ON THE JUNKER SINGLE-SEATER ALL-METAL MONOPLANE, TYPE D.I.

The aeroplane forming the subject of the report was examined at Evère Aerodrome, near Brussels. Its earlier history is unknown, but the fuselage showed clearly that it had been struck by several bursts of machine gun bullets.

The evidence for its classification as a D.I. model is mentioned under the heading " Painting."

While the aerodynamic design is interesting, the constructional features are judged to be of great importance. The machine is entirely constructed of metal, is unarmoured, and carries still further the positive system of control and the elimination of cables noticed in the case of the biplane.

It may be mentioned, in passing, that the machine had been dumped in the open, and had shared the varied weather of several months with other machines constructed of wood and fabric materials. The Junker had hardly suffered, while the orthodox type of machine had seriously deteriorated. In some places, however, the duralumin sheet was covered with a thin coating of white crystals, and appeared to have become brittle.

GENERAL PARTICULARS.

Type of machine	D.I. monoplane.
Purpose	Single-seater fighter.
Engine	180 h.p. Mercedes.
Span	29 ft. 2 in.
Overall length	22 ft. 0 in.
Chord (at root of wings)	5 ft. 11½ in.
Maximum height (estimated)	9 ft. 5 in.
Maximum cross-sectional area of body	9·25 sq. ft.
Airscrew	(Axial; pitch, 2,150 mm. Diameter, 2,740 mm.
Area of each wing (with aileron, as far as junction with centre section)	73·6 sq. ft.
Area of one aileron	10·25 sq. ft.
Area of centre section (one side)	5·8 sq. ft.
Total supporting surface (both sides)	158·8 sq. ft.
Area of fixed tail planes (both sides)	12·2 sq. ft.
Area of elevator	18·2 sq. ft.
Area of rudder (estimated)	8·2 sq. ft.
Horizontal area of fuselage	36·8 sq. ft.
Vertical area of fuselage	64·5 sq. ft.

WINGS, GENERAL DESIGN.

The Junker monoplane presents, at first sight, the appearance of a biplane with the upper plane removed, the wings being found where the lower plane of a biplane is usually fitted. There is a short horizontal centre section which is built up integrally with the body, and which contains seven tubular spars.

To each side of this section is attached a plane, which is shaped as shown in the general arrangement drawings. The dihedral angle is adjustable; the evidence of a German photograph indicates a dihedral angle of 3 deg. on the upper surface of the wings. There is no sweep back.

WING CONSTRUCTION.

In its broad outlines the construction of the planes of the monoplane is similar to that of the biplane wings. In both Junker machines the designer has separated himself completely from the influence due to the use of the wood spars and ribs that are almost universally employed in a non-metal wing construction, and has set out to use his new material in the best possible way. Instead of two main spars crossed more or less at right angles by built-up ribs, the construction described and illustrated below has resulted.

A series of tubular duralumin spars are strongly braced by means of riveted duralumin cross-pieces, and to the frame thus formed is riveted a corrugated sheet covering, also of duralumin.

The difference lies in the fact that, whereas in the biplane the interspar bracing is of duralumin tubes (except at the extreme tips, where strips are substituted), in the monoplane wings strips are used throughout the length of the plane.

The bracing strips are all similar in shape, but vary in length and thickness of metal according to position. Near the root the thickness is ·033 (about 21 S.W.G.). The section drawn in Fig. 1 is only found in the middle portion of the strip. From

FIG. 1 (ACTUAL SIZE).

this section the strips gradually flatten out, so that at the extremities, where they are riveted to the spars, they are practically flat.

The arrangement of the bracing is worthy of attention. Each of the three upper spars is connected to the two adjacent lower spars in such a manner as to form a Warren girder, and the upper apices coincide, so that the arrangement may be otherwise described as a series of alternately inverted square pyramids of bracing strips.

Photograph 2 will explain this, and will show that no bracing strips are found between any two adjacent upper spars or between any two adjacent lower spars.

FIG. 2.

It will be understood, therefore, that the corrugated covering completes the system of triangulation upon which the strength of the structure depends.

The seven spars are parallel throughout their whole length so far as the plan view is concerned, but converge so that at the wing tip their extremities are almost in line.

The wing section, taken at the wing root, is drawn to scale in Fig. 3, and on this diagram are marked the various letters that are referred to from time to time in this description. From this point the section tapers consistently to the tips. The channel section piece marked A (24 S.W.G., 25 mm. wide and 15 cm. deep) may be

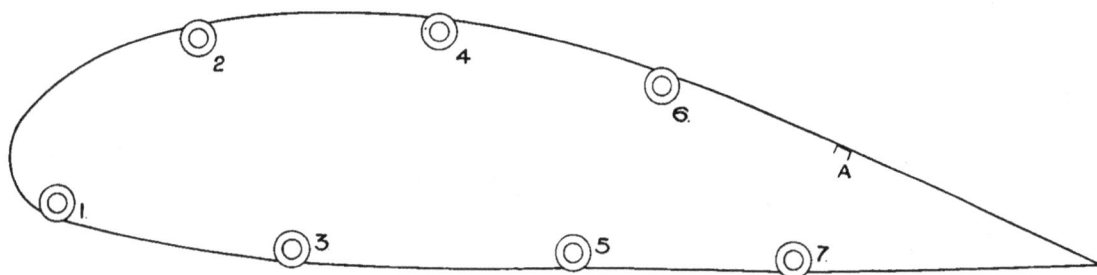

FIG. 3.

regarded as an eighth spar, but it does not extend from end to end of the wing. It finishes at the bulkhead marked B in Fig. 2. This bulkhead, consisting of a channel sheet of aluminium, performs several important functions. Primarily, it supports the hinge necessary to the working of the aileron control, but it also closes the triangular gap which would otherwise be left where the aileron commences. It is attached by riveted strips to the spars numbered 5 and 6 in Fig. 3, and is, of course, roughly triangular in shape. The metal is of 20 S.W.G. The shape of the aileron is made clear in the scale drawings, and it will be noticed that its accommodation does not necessitate interference with any of the tubular spars. It is hinged to a channel section spar, which is lightened by circular holes, and which is inclined at an angle to the wing spars. Four parallel strips lie along the lower surface of the wing, and connect the roots of each of the four lower spars to the aileron bulkhead or to the trailing edge. Each is of 24 S.W.G. duralumin, 48 mm. wide, and is riveted at 10 cm. intervals to the lower wing covering.

Between spars 1 and 3, and also between spars 3 and 5, two waved section strips, each 45 mm. wide, and of 29 S.W.G. duralumin, are riveted to the inside of the lower covering parallel to the spars. These are all plainly visible in Fig. 2.

All of the seven tubular spars are spliced. In the case of the upper spars the splice occurs 1 m. 59 cm. from the root, and the diameter decreases from 45 mm. to 40 mm. The lower spar splices are found 1 m. 27 cm. from the root, and the spar diameters before and after splice are 35 mm. and 30 mm. respectively.

The splices are similar to those described in connection with the Junker biplane but, owing to the fact that the outside diameter of the inner tube is not very much less than the internal diameter of the outer one, it has not been found necessary to press the outside tube to a square section. Arrows marked in Fig. 2 show four of the splices.

The outer extremities of the spars are received in a channel strip, which follows the junction of the corrugated covering and the riveted-on edge found at the wing tips. (See Fig. 4.) The spars pass through holes in this strip, and are cut off squarely

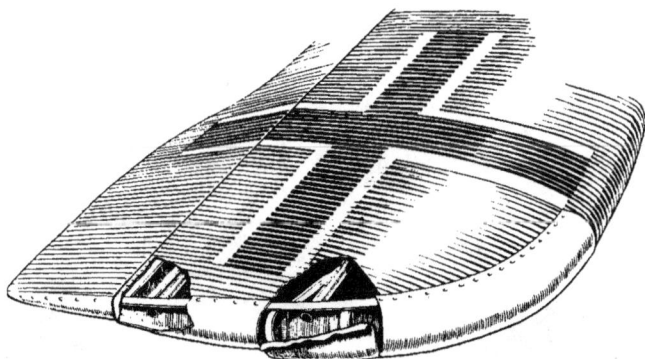

FIG. 4.

an inch or two beyond it. The ends are left open, and small angle pieces are riveted to spar and strip to complete the joint. The separate wing tip is a substantial duralumin sheet (of 20 S.W.G.), riveted to the channel strip, and between these two the corrugated wing covering is firmly held. At intervals D-shaped duralumin formers of 24 S.W.G. are riveted to strip and edge.

It is only at the tip that a separate edge is found. The wing covering consists of corrugated sheet duralumin, ·014 in. thick (about 24 S.W.G.). The pitch of corrugation is 1¼ in. and the depth $\frac{3}{16}$ in., of which there are seven strips lap-riveted together. Each strip forms a belt, commencing at the trailing edge and passing right round the wing back to the trailing edge, where the two edges are riveted together. Spars and covering are joined by iron rivets spaced in the hollows of the waves. The two channel pieces—one acting as aileron spar and the other receiving the ends of the spars—meet and are riveted together at the wing corner.

CENTRE SECTION CONSTRUCTION AND SPAR JOINTS.

The bracing of the centre section, however, is exactly similar to that of the Junker biplane; that is, the spars are connected by means of duralumin tubes, which are flattened at each extremity, and riveted to lugs welded to steel collars, which are in turn riveted to the spars. Various photographs (particularly Figs. 5 and 6) show clearly the character and disposition of this bracing. The tubes are of 20 mm. outside diameter, and the metal of 18 S.W.G.

FIG. 5.

FIG. 6.

The seven tubular spars terminate in screw collar joints, somewhat similar to those reported upon in connection with the Junker biplane, but are sufficiently different to merit description.

The junction of upper spar to upper spar is drawn to scale in Fig. 7. Instead of being immovably riveted to the spar, as is the case in the J.I. biplane, the internal

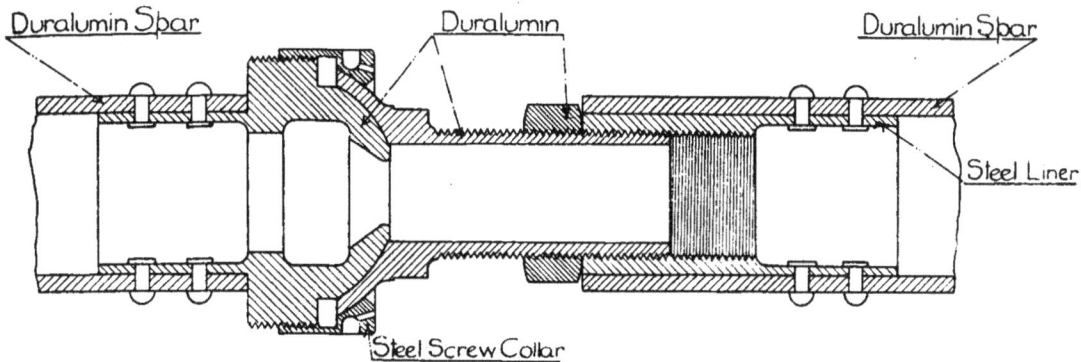

FIG. 7.

sleeve which carries the partly-spherical head is threaded, and screwed into the spar. By this means the effective length of the upper spars can be varied to the extent of several inches. The junction of the four lower spars to the corresponding tubes of the centre section is exactly similar to that employed in the case of the biplane, and is not adjustable.

This arrangement obviously allows the angle of dihedral of the planes to be capable of alteration within certain wide limits, and at the same time provides a joint of ample strength. The drawing shows which parts are of duralumin, and which of steel.

AILERONS.

The unbalanced ailerons pivot on axes which are not quite parallel to the leading edge of the wing. They are built up in the simplest possible way. A duralumin tube forms the aileron spar, and to this two separate corrugated sheets are riveted, one above and one below. At the rear the two sheets are riveted together, and a D-shaped duralumin sheet, without corrugations, is riveted on to form a leading edge, and so serves to bridge the gap between aileron and plane. There are no formers or ribs in the ailerons.

The three hinges are of the usual construction, steel collars with welded-on lugs being pinned to the aileron spar. Corresponding lugs are riveted to the channel section strip mentioned in the wing description.

FUSELAGE.

The body of the D.I. monoplane differs entirely in construction from that of the biplane. Ignoring for the moment the front armoured portion of the biplane fuselage, the construction of the rear part goes only one step further than that of the usual German metal tube fuselage.

The usual wire bracing (found in the metal-tube bodies of the Fokker and A.E.G. machines) is replaced by rigid tubular bracing. The designer of the monoplane, however, has evidently based the fuselage upon the familiar German construction, wherein a framework of wood longerons is covered with one or more skins of 3-ply, and wherein wire bracing is entirely absent; and not being hampered by the necessity of arranging for armour plating, he has been able to build a metal fuselage on sound " framework-and-covering-sans-bracing " lines.

Generally speaking, the body consists of a framework of duralumin formers, covered by a single riveted-on skin of sheet duralumin corrugated lengthwise.

Reference to the side-view in the scale drawings will show that the position of the built-up formers is revealed by double lines (dotted). To the rear of the pilot's seat two single dotted lines are equally spaced between each pair of double lines. These represent strips of duralumin, having a waved section, which are riveted to the covering. They are simply strips, and are not built up or braced in any way.

The rivets are of aluminium, and are placed where the hollows of the strip wave touch the hollows of the covering wave. The body finishes abruptly, immediately in front of the tail, and between this rear end and the bulkhead behind the pilot there is no construction other than the built-up formers, the strip formers, and the covering. The covering thus constitutes an important factor in the fuselage construction, and takes a larger share in the strengthening of the body than does the 3-ply of a wood fuselage, where substantial longerons are generally employed. It is true that in the Junker a continuous channel section strip runs longitudinally along the top and bottom of the fuselage, thus serving to connect the various formers. This strip is so frail, however, that its obvious function is to assist in the assembly of the body by holding the formers in place while the covering is riveted on. It takes no substantial place in the actual construction.

The analogy between the 3-ply construction and this metal body will now be evident—in both cases the covering is called upon to take an important share in the strength of the structure, in contradistinction to being a mere covering or fairing.

The lengthwise corrugations naturally stiffen the covering against strains tending to bend the body of the machine, and enable the skin to be the only factor in the construction which does perform this function. The strong cross bulkheads provide stiffness in the direction of the covering's greatest weakness, i.e., against strains tending to deform the cross-section of the body. Thus, between the two a very rigid structure is obtained. A further analysis of the comparison and contrast between 3-ply and metal construction leads one to realise that the corrugations take the place of the wood longerons found in the 3-ply system.

Fore Part of Fuselage.—The simple construction of the fuselage is modified forward of the pilot's cockpit. To allow the necessary elbow-room for the pilot, it has been necessary to eliminate one bulkhead, and the space between the former, just behind the pilot, and the one immediately behind the engine—a distance of nearly 4 ft.—is braced with a scheme of triangulated channel-section strips, which are riveted to the inside of the fuselage skin. The side view of the machine given in the scale drawings shows quite clearly the system employed. The cross strains here are taken by the wing spars, the tube supporting the front of the pilot's seat, and the wind-screen support. This last is of L-section steel, of fairly heavy gauge.

The foundation of the construction forward of the cockpit is provided by the centre section wing spars. The middle of the three upper spars forms the bottom

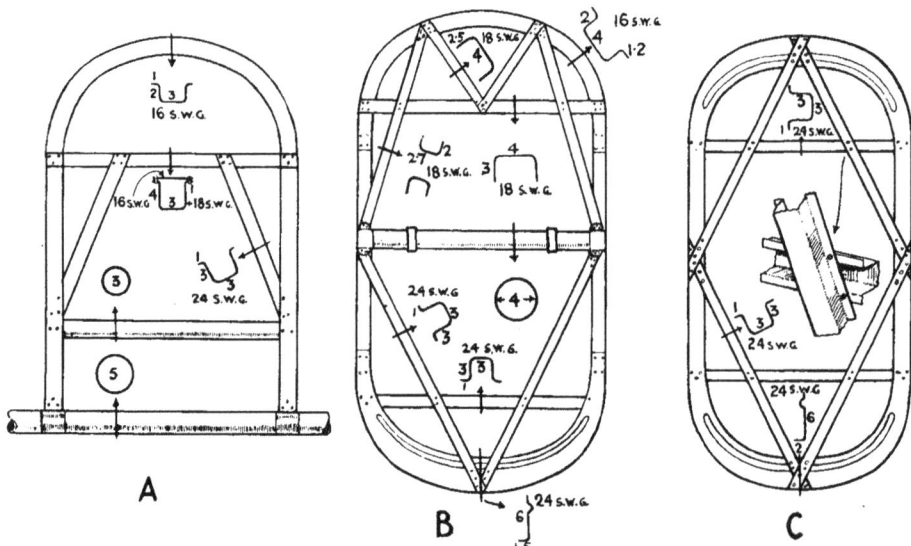

Fig. 8 (A, B & C).

of the first cross former, drawn in Fig. 8 (A), and in Fig. 9 is shown, diagrammatically, the system of tubular bracing which supports the engine bearers. All the joints are made on the same principle. A steel collar is riveted round the duralumin tube to which other tubes are to be attached, and lugs welded on wherever these tubes finish; their extremities are flattened and riveted directly to the lugs. Most of the tubes are of 18 S.W.G., and of 20 mm. outside diameter

The Bulkheads.—Fig. 8 (A) is a diagram of the bulkhead behind the engine—it also figures in Fig. 9. The various cross-sections and gauges are marked.

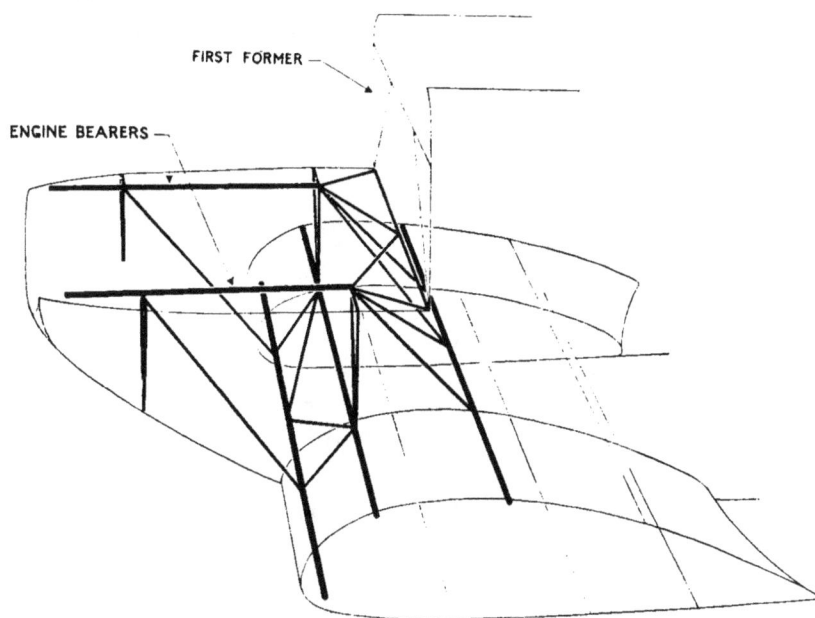

FIRST FORMER —

ENGINE BEARERS —

Fig. 9.

Fig. 8 (B) is a diagram of the former immediately behind the pilot. The flat-sided oval which constitutes the outside framework is of channel-section duralumin, with flanges for riveting, and is in four portions. The top part extends to the line just below the upper cross-bar, and is of 16 S.W.G. as marked. The figures placed near the various sides of the cross-section represent the lengths of those sides in centimetres. The two straight side pieces are of similar cross-section, but of 20 S.W.G. metal, while the lower portion is of 24 S.W.G. metal, with the cross-section indicated. Across the middle a 4 cm. o.d. duralumin tube passes, and is riveted at the ends to the side pieces. Above and below this tube, and parallel to it, two strips are riveted in position; the respective sections are shown. The lower half is braced by a Vee as indicated, and this is the normal bracing for each half in other bulkheads. The bracing is modified, however, in the upper half, and takes the form of a letter M, the reason being that the peculiar inverted U seen on the top of the fuselage, just to the rear of the pilot, is attached to the two upper points of the M. It will be noticed that the side limbs of the M are each composed of two similar strips.

The next bulkhead is 50 cm. behind, and is shown diagrammatically in Fig. 8 (C). It has no central cross tube, but has the usual diamond of bracing strips. Sections, sizes and gauges are shown.

Between these two are found the two waved section strips mentioned above. The next three bulkheads (Nos. 4, 5 and 6) do not differ from this one except in dimensions, and each pair is separated by two waved strips. The seventh former is the last one of the fuselage bulkhead, and is modified to accommodate the four points of attachment of tail portion to body. Fig. 10 is a photograph of this bulkhead, and incidentally shows many of the points already described.

The rear detachable portion of the body is dealt with under the head "Tail unit."

Fuselage Covering.—The pitch of the corrugations is about $1\frac{1}{4}$ in., and the depth about ·33 in. The thickness is ·015 in. (about 28 S.W.G.), except the engine cowls, which are ·01 in. thick.

Five sheets are employed, each without joint from front to rear—

(1) One sheet covering the bottom of the body.
(2) and (3) Two symmetrical side sheets.
(4) and (5) Two symmetrical top sheets.

In addition, two smaller sheets serve as port and starboard engine cowls. The lines of junction are shown in the scale drawings.

External and Internal Fuselage Fittings.—The corrugated covering is continuous from the rear to the front of the body, except that hinged cowls cover the engine on each side. Over the front portion of the wings may be seen (in several photographs) rectangular holes which were originally covered by sheet duralumin doors. They are intended, of course, to allow access to the engine sump, etc. Examina-

FIG. 10.

tion of Fig. 5 will reveal a stirrup to facilitate entry into the cockpit. This is found on the port side only, and is constructed of stout duralumin tube, riveted to the side by means of two bent strips of duralumin. Directly behind the pilot may be seen a kind of pylon, which is clearly visible in several illustrations. This is very strongly constructed of stout steel tubes, welded together. Its function cannot be named with certainty, but it is highly probable that it is intended to save the pilot in the event of the machine overturning. It is possible that a certain amount of reluctance to fly all-metal machines was evinced by pilots, and this is probably a concession to them. A little to the rear of the black cross painted on the fuselage, and in line with its horizontal component, there is on each side of the body a small rectangular door. These doors give access to the swinging support of the elevator control tube described later.

Handles for lifting the tail of the machine while on the ground are fitted at the rear of the body at either side. Their construction is exactly similar to that of the step, and their exact position is revealed in the photographs.

The pilot's seat is constructed of corrugated duralumin riveted to a channel-section framework, and clipped to the bulkhead immediately behind. Its position is not adjustable. The bulkhead just mentioned—the one directly behind the pilot —is made airtight by the fact that a piece of fabric is held between bulkhead and skin by the rivets employed to hold both together.

CONTROLS.

The D.I. Junker carries a stage further the tendency towards positive control lately evident in German machines. Both aileron and elevator are operated by steel tubes, and only the rudder control is by cable. It may be mentioned, in passing, that these cables are the only ones that could be found anywhere on the machine.

The head of the control lever is shown in Fig. 11. It will be noticed that the left-hand grip constitutes a throttle control, the idea of the two handles probably being to ensure that at any opening of the throttle one of the grips shall be in a convenient position. The two machine gun controls are also clearly shown.

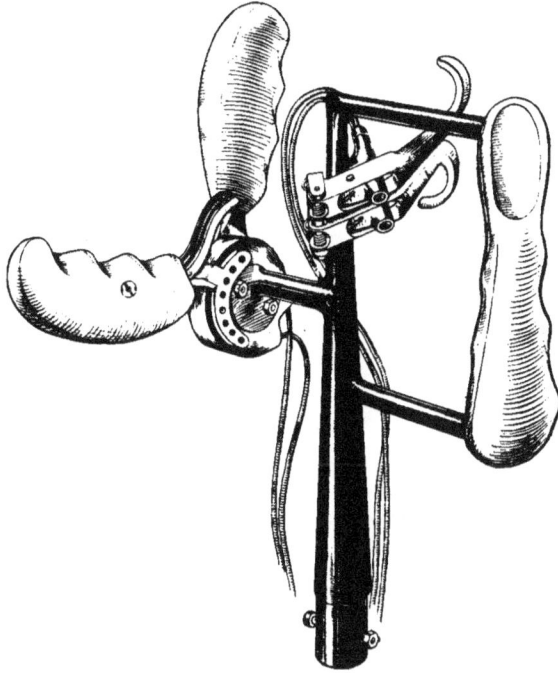

FIG. 11.

Fig. 12 gives a clear idea of the general control arrangements. The joy-stick has a welded steel triangular base, and is pivoted on a bolt, which forms the base of the triangle. Parallel vertical lugs, each carrying five holes, are welded on what roughly corresponds to the apex of the triangle, and in one pair of these holes the eye-boat is hinged which forms one extremity of the elevator-control tube. So far as this elevator-control is concerned, therefore, two kinds of adjustment are possible. Firstly, the actual length of the compression tube between joy-stick and elevator

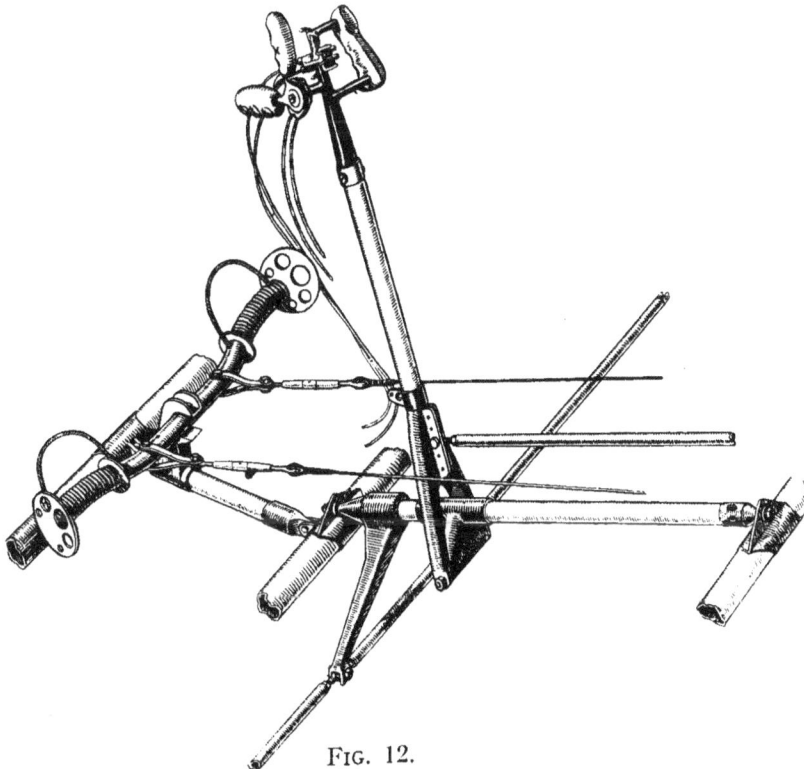

FIG. 12.

king-post is adjustable. This, apart from the purely mechanical considerations involved, allows the relation between joy-stick and elevator to be varied within

C

certain limits, so that when the joy-stick is vertical it does not necessarily follow that the elevator is neutral. Secondly, the five holes on the joy-stick allow of an adjustment of gearing between joy-stick and elevator, so that this latter may be arranged to move through five different angles for the same amount of movement of the joy-stick.

Fig. 13 (c) is a sketch of the elevator king-post, and in Fig. 10 may be seen the

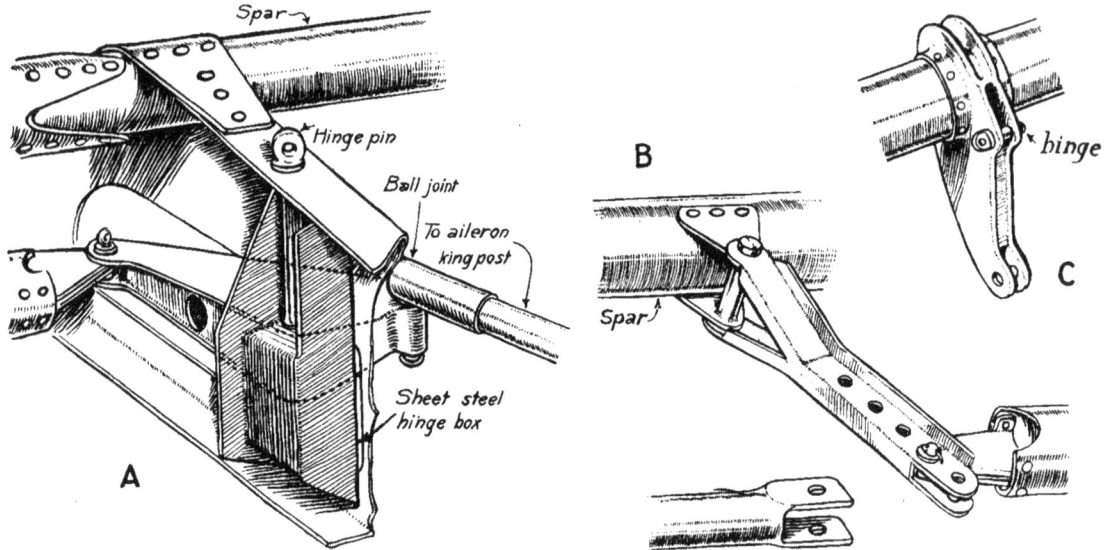

FIG. 13 (A, B, & C).

swinging support for the elevator-control tube. Owing to the two converging pieces being broken off, the exact type of joint used cannot be ascertained.

The aileron control is particularly interesting, and may be understood more clearly by referring to Fig. 14. It will be seen that a lateral movement of the

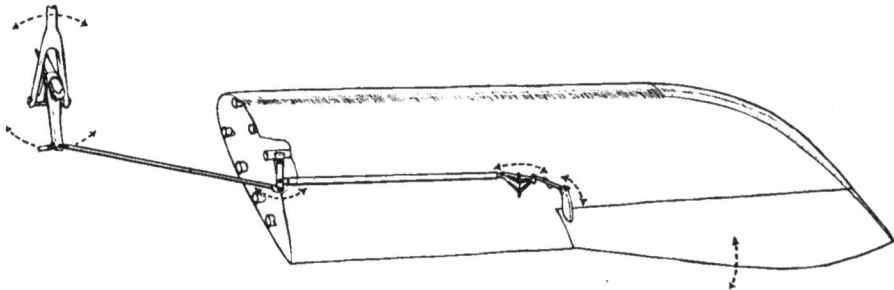

FIG. 14.

control lever actuates a longitudinal rocking shaft, which carries a downward pointing arm, forked at its lower extremity. Between the jaws of the fork are pivoted the extremities of two light steel tubes of 20 mm. diameter, which pass one through each half of the centre section, and finish in fork ends. The length of these tubes is adjustable at the inner ends, and the welded joins, which constitute the outer ends, are bolted to a short arm pivoted in turn to the rearmost of the three upper spars, about 6 in. from the root. This arm has five pairs of holes to accommodate the ends of two tubes—the control tube already described as passing from joy-stick to the arm, and another second tube passing inside the wing, vertically under the upper rear wing spar. This second tube is of duralumin (diameter 35 mm.), and its outer extremity is pinned to a kind of bell crank, to the upper point of which is fitted a short steel tube connecting bell crank and aileron king-post. It is evident that this steel tube must work at right angles to the wing spars, and to allow for this change of direction, the joint between bell crank and steel tube is of the ball and socket type.

The adjustment of the gearing between control lever and aileron is effected by means of the five holes in the pivoted arm. The number of possible variations in gearing is as many as twenty, but not all of these come within the range of practical utility. The diagrams marked Fig. 13 show the mechanical details of the aileron control, (A) being the hinge, (B) the pivoted arm, and (C) the elevator king-post.

The rudder bar is of the conventional type (*see* Fig. 12) and is made of steel tubing. Cables connect the bar with the rudder king-post, so that the rudder control does not depart in any particular from the usual system.

TAIL UNIT.

This portion of the Junker D.I. is particularly interesting, and incorporates several novel features. The corrugated fuselage covering finishes in a vertical plane just in front of the tail planes, and a rear body portion is built up integrally with the fixed tail planes.

The construction of this tail portion follows the general lines laid down for the front part of the fuselage. Immediately behind the front edge a strong bulkhead is built up, and this frame carries the tail part of the attachments. This bulkhead, No. 8, is clearly shown in Fig. 15, which also shows a horizontal duralumin tube,

FIG. 15.

supported a few inches in front of the bulkhead by means of four channel-section strips, which connect the extremities of the tubes to the bulkhead, two above and two below.

It should be borne in mind that this tube, though attached to the eighth former, becomes part of the seventh former when the tail portion is fitted to the body.

The ninth and last former is behind No. 8, and a diagram is shown in Fig. 16. It is to the upper portion of this former that the rudder post bearing is riveted. It consists of a bronze bush, about 17 cm. long, which is welded, by means of brazed-on steel collars, to a shaped piece of stout sheet steel, which is, in turn, riveted to the bulkhead. Fig. 17 shows this construction.

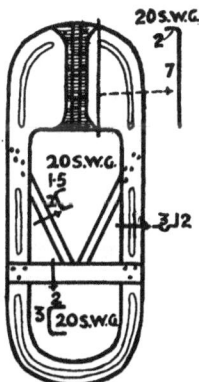

FIG. 16.

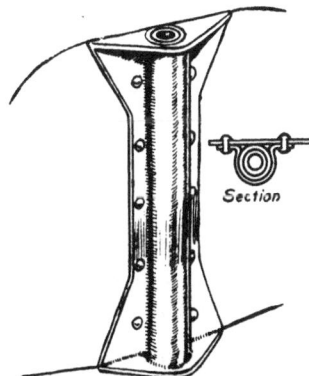

FIG. 17.

JUNCTION OF BODY AND TAIL.

Fig. 18, which is a diagram intended only to show the method of joining, shows the four-point attachment, but omits all details of bulkhead construction, etc.

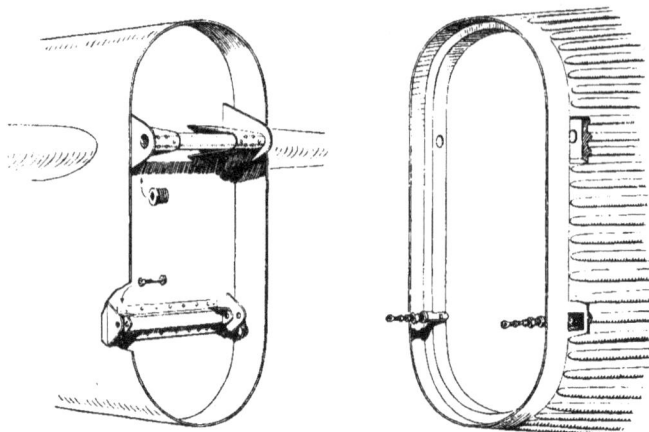

FIG. 18.

The horizontal duralumin tube mentioned above, as being fixed to the eighth bulkhead, carries threaded steel liners into which special hollow nuts screw. This arrangement provides what amounts to a pivot round which the tail portion can be swung (before, of course, the nuts are tightened up). The two lower attachments are really adjustable links—one is drawn half actual size in Fig. 19. It will be observed that, by means of a left-handed thread and a right-handed one, a considerable amount of variation is possible.

FIG. 19.

Since the tail planes are built into the tail portion, it is clear that the amount of this variation determines the angle of incidence of the tail planes. The shape of the rear portion gives an excellent streamline finish to the fuselage, and there is sufficient overlap between the coverings of body and tail-piece to ensure there being no gap at any reasonable setting of the rear portion.

The fixed tail planes have a strong riveted-on leading edge, to which the corrugated covering is attached.

Fig. 20, which serves to amplify this description, shows that the corrugations of the covering begin immediately behind the leading edge, which proves that this covering has been specially corrugated to suit its specific position, and is not just a piece cut from a larger corrugated sheet. A duralumin spar passes from side to side of the tail in the position shown by several of the photographs. It is a built-up spar, consisting of two channel section pieces, connected by two systems of Warren bracing, one on each side. At the rear of the tail planes is another channel spar, with its open side pointing rearward, and it is to this spar that the elevator is hinged, by means similar to those already described in connection with the aileron. The tail covering is connected to the fuselage covering by a separate right-angled strip riveted to both. The tail construction is further strengthened by two strips on each side of the body similar to those used for wing bracing. These are plainly visible in Fig. 20.

The single elevator is balanced, and is constructed very simply. There are no ribs or formers, but the covering is riveted directly to the hinge tube, which passes from end to end of the elevator. Narrow curved strips of duralumin are riveted above and below, and serve to bridge the gap between elevator and tail planes.

The D-shaped leading edge of the tail is carried on along the tips of the elevator, but the trailing edge is composed simply of the upper and lower coverings riveted together.

FIG. 20,

The tail skid is of ash, with the usual steel shoe. It is pivoted near its middle, the pivoting bolt being carried in a strong steel cradle, covered by an aluminium fairing. The shock-absorber is of triple-coil spring, and is attached to each side of the fuselage, as shown in Fig. 10.

ENGINE.

The 180 H.P. Mercedes engine bears the number 36975, and was guaranteed till 11th June, 1918. It is supported upon channel section bearers (4 cm. by 4 cm., open at top, 12 S.W.G. duralumin), which are wood-filled from the front end to within 10 cm. of the rear. These bearers are carried on a triangulated system of duralumin tubes, flattened at the extremities and riveted to steel collars, as was described in the report on the Junker biplane. In this system the wing spars, which are continuous throughout the centre section, play a leading part.

The propeller is an Axial, No. 18646, and bears this inscription :—

18646.
Axial.
Edul. Zug.
160 P.S. D.274 St.215.
T.P. 90 G.

which gives the diameter as 2,740 mm., and the pitch as 2,150 mm.

It is built up of the usual laminations, and fixed to the crankshaft by the customary eight bolts.

PETROL SYSTEM.

It is probable that two separate petrol tanks were carried in the centre section, one on either side. They must have been accommodated in the triangular space between the bracing tubes. In Fig. 6 there may be seen a flat steel strip, bent round, with its two ends connected by a turnbuckle. This indicates that the tanks were probably cylindrical in form. The fact that the bracing tubes, which would be in contact with the tanks, are bound with coarse fabric tends to confirm the placing of the tanks.

Fig. 21 is a diagram of the dashboard of the Junker, with translated inscriptions. The dash itself consists of two separate aluminium sheets as shown, with discs crudely inscribed. The actual cocks had been removed. The evidence of the inscriptions is obvious.

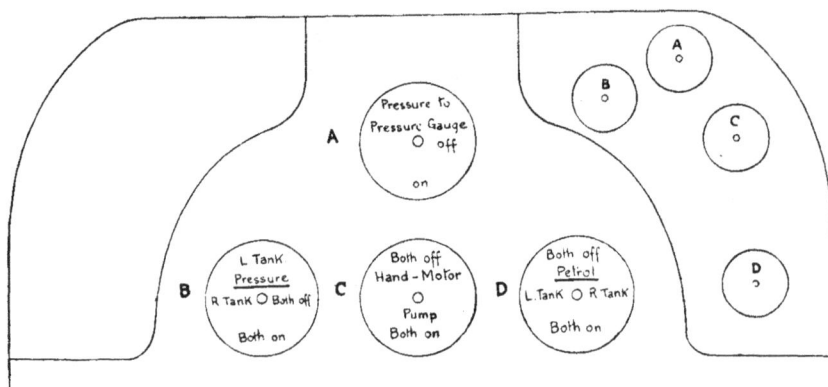

FIG. 21.

RADIATOR.

It is evident from the photographs, and from various traces that still remain on the machine, that two separate half-radiators were fitted, one on each side of the engine, at the front of the fuselage. (*See* view of complete machine.)

The positive shutter control can still be traced from the pilot's seat to each half-radiator.

PAINTING.

The body is painted a chocolate-brown colour, except underneath, where a white pigment has been applied. The wings are painted a pale green, with irregular patches of light mauve on top, and white underneath. The tail planes and elevator are white above and below.

Close examination revealed the fact that under the layer of chocolate paint on the body was a layer of pale green colour, and a similar colour could be seen on the tail planes wherever the white had peeled off. The chocolate and white were all flat, unvaried colour. Careful scrutiny of the fuselage side revealed the fact that on the top of the green colour, on the starboard side, the inscription " JUNK.D.I." had been painted—the slightly-raised edges of the latters could just be traced. This had been obliterated by the chocolate paint, but is important as evidence that a German single-seater fighter may be put in the " D " class, whether monoplane or biplane. On the other hand is the case of the Fokker monoplane, also a single-seater fighter, known by the old-style classification E. (for eindecker ; *i.e.,* monoplane).

ARMAMENT.

The photographs show two Spandau guns, fixed on channel duralumin bearers, immediately in front of the pilot. They are fired in the usual manner through interrupter gears controlled from the joystick. Nothing unusual was noticed with regard to the aluminium chutes and ammunition magazines.

G. T. C. (Ap. D.(L)).

R. BROOKE-POPHAM,
Brigadier-General,
Director of Research.

July, 1919.

FIG. 22.

FIG. 23.

FIG. 24.

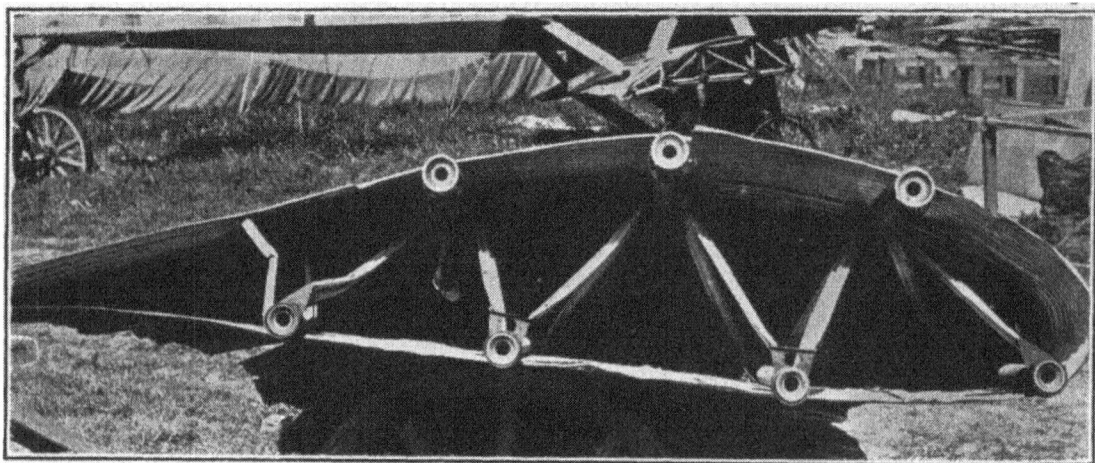

FIG. 25.　VIEW LOOKING INTO THE PORT WING.

FIG. 26.　THE STARBOARD SIDE OF THE DISMANTLED AEROPLANE.

www.ingramcontent.com/pod-product-compliance
Lightning Source LLC
Chambersburg PA
CBHW081543090426
42741CB00014BA/3254